I KILLED MY

GIANT

IN STILETTOS

By,
Katavah L. Walker

I Killed My Giant in Stilettos
Katavah L. Walker

Books can be ordered through booksellers or by contacting:

Katavah L. Walker Ministries at
katavahwalker@gmail.com

For more information, visit our Facebook page at:
www.facebook.com/katavahwalkermin

ISBN-13: 978-0-692-08151-8
ISBN-10: 0692081518

Dedication

*This book is dedicated to all the people who allow
"fear" to grip them in ways that distract them from
becoming what God intended for their life. Kill
"fear" as you work your vision…don't sit and wait
for it to go away.*

Step (1) Acknowledge that it exists.

*Step (2) Research tools to help you understand the
giant you are faced with and how you will conquer it
or them.*

*Step (3) Face it, defeat it, kill it, and encourage
someone else to do the same.*

*(Ladies, find your favorite pair of stilettos and let's
kill some giants!)*

Love ya,

Katavah L. Walker

Acknowledgements

God, the creator from whom all blessings flow, I honor you this day. To your son, Jesus Christ, who has blessed me beyond measure, I praise you forever and always.

To my parents, Bishop Steve and Marilyn "Sis. Honey" Lester, you two are amazing. Thank you for bringing me up fearing God and turning me in the direction that I should go. My two sisters, Kizmat (Jamal) Tention and Koddi (Wade) Lester-Dunn, my handsome nephew Steven and my diva Anaya, and the crew, let's see Stevanie, Akira, Stevon, Nigerra, Jeremiah, Jaden-Christopher and Jordyn-Taylor (my boo) ...WOW! I love you all!

To my family Anthony Wright (father) and two sisters Tina and Tiffany, I love you dearly.

To my princess Krishae`A. Walker, your name in Hebrew, "gifted and favored by God". You are my sunshine on a rainy day. You are the twinkle in the star. You are smart, you are important, and you are kind, but you definitely have your own twist... but I love you Light Skin!!! Lol!

To my Greater Grace family, you all know I love each and every one of you. This little church on the corner of Bank Street, y'all got my heart. To my church mother, Reba Pace, you are my strength. To our newly appointed assistant pastor, Henry Pitts and family, our finance committee, my other mother from way back, Shelia Barbara, all the Elders, Missionaries, musicians, the Board of Directors, Pastor's Aide, ushers, greeters, media and last but not least, the Levites of Praise (singers)...thank you for your hard work and all your sacrifices.

Wiping my forehead, I think that covered everyone...LOL.

To Granny Lucile Lester and Grandma Dolly B. Foster my two favorite girls!!!

Rest in Heaven Nancy Long, Lela Bell Arnold & Mary Ann Harper... I love you!

To my heart, my boo, my Pillow...Larq Womble. As you endeavor on the roads ahead, stay focused, keep God as the center of your life and there's nothing you can't accomplish. #20 #mysongbird

To my squad, Margot Brown, girl, you da truth...my travel agent, my baby's god mama and so much more. Cassandra Williams (mother), you are gifted in prayer and I thank you for every one of them. And Nicole Alexander...my, what a story we have. You keep me grounded at times and on my face at others... but you're my girl. Thank you for editing this book and walking me through the publishing process. It's no wonder that you're studying Mental Health Counseling because I think I was her first client in more ways than one.

To my Spiritual Sisters in the gospel to name a few...

Evangelist Oma Wright (my baby's other god mama), Evangelist Cherrise Stephens, Co-Pastor Judy Russell, Co-Pastor Laurona Phelps, Pastor Stacey Walker Alexander, Pastor Shuntray Sheddrick, Evangelist Plezie Smalls, Apostle Deborah Sheppard, Pastor Crystal Lewis, Evangelist Michelle Martin, and Evangelist Cheryl Twilley (my boo).

To my god sister Iris M. McNeil (congrats on your first born), god sons Myles Brown, Greg "Sticks" Twilley, and god daughters Nyasia Richardson (New Haven), Breydan and Chloe'.

To the ladies of Level 8, it's so much to say but know that I love you all... on many different levels. Devi Hawkins-Prather (committed and diva), Sharon Graham (compassionate and dedicated), Darlene Harper (care-giver and the best cook all around), LeAndrea Williams (quiet but focused), Tameka Burse-Farrier (bossy and driven) and Charlene Davis (business lady and advisor).

Lol!!!! Almost done.

Bishop Norman O. Harper & First Lady Arabella Harper, South Central Georgia Jurisdiction, the late Mother Edith L McGrew, Dr. Sandra Ervin, Mrs. Carolyn Rickards-Williams, Sis. Hilda Dillon and newly appointed principal to Zion Baptist Academy Dr. George Weathers.

To my staff at Zion Baptist Academy…Ms. Che` loves all of you.

To my angel, Marsha Alexander, I love you mama.

To my big brother B. Chase Williams and ShaBach family…I love y'all still.

Anyone out there, if you run into Queen Latifah, please tell her I need to meet her asap… lol!

Last but certainly not least…

2K was a good year for me. That was the year I married my friend. We were introduced in January and by December, I had a new last name. You were everything I prayed for…tall, dark, handsome, intelligent, saved and had no kids. Well, 17 years later, you're still tall, dark, handsome, intelligent, saved and we have one daughter. You're a phenomenal pastor and mentor. You think you're my financial advisor who can tell me how to spend my money (lol) but for real…you are the saver of the family. You're a man of wisdom, strength and leadership, a provider, and I thank you for listening to me with all my craziness. You may be soft spoken but yet have a spirit of a fearless lion.

Pastor Walker, I appreciate all the love and support. I thank you for your patience during this journey, through the long nights and weekends of pulling my thoughts together as I was creating chapters. I thank you for never questioning my dreams or my purpose. I don't know how many times I interrupted family time to have sofa time, talking out these pages. But you always pushed me and told me to stay focused and do what God said do. You've encouraged me for years to step out but because of "fear", I pushed others to work on their visions and write their books instead of focusing on mine. I helped other ministries build. I carried and supported conferences, workshops and revivals, I was the mistress of ceremony, I was the crowd hype woman and the name that drew people. I was often looked down on, maybe because I wasn't driving the latest vehicle, wearing designer clothes, or even hanging around the popular women preachers whose names were on every flyer. But as my husband, you always said, if I was happy doing what I was doing, then do it with a grateful heart.

So, I publicly acknowledge you, my husband, pastor and friend...Pastor Christopher C. Walker, I love you and thank you for being you! To your parents, Pastor Grover C. Walker and Elsie Seldon, without you two, well...

God bless, and may His love continue to rest, rule and abide in you daily.

Now let's start this easy read. May each page uncover a giant in you that you are ready to kill so you can go and do greater!

TABLE OF CONTENTS

Six Inches in a Bag

One of the most familiar stories in the Bible is that of David and Goliath. Most people who have attended at least one Sunday School class or heard a bedtime Bible story could tell you that the young, sheepherder David shocked everyone by killing the giant Philistine with a slingshot and a stone to the head. We tell the story to our children to teach them there's no situation too big that we can't handle with God on our side, but there are some details that as adults we don't always remember or focus on.

The first thing that comes to light when David sees and hears about Goliath, is a question that he asked the other men who were shying away in fear. He asked, "What shall be done for the man who kills this Philistine and takes away the reproach from Israel?". David was informed that the man who killed the giant would receive great riches from the king, the king's daughter's hand in marriage and would be exempt from taxes in Israel. What if David had been told that the winner of the fight would receive nothing more than the thrill of victory? Would his decision to risk his life have been the same if the reward wasn't as great? I believe the answer to his question changed the course of David's day and fueled his determination to even attempt to kill the giant. In that moment, David made the decision that what was possible for him to possess was worth more than the fear that paralyzed others. His future lied in the defeat of this giant!

Oftentimes the frustrations of life are compounded because we either waste energy fighting giants that are irrelevant to our future and have no reward for us as individuals, or we allow the giants that directly affect our future to render us powerless because of fear. But like David, we can make the choice to take hold of our future and kill the giants that stand in our way.

The next thing about the story of David that seems to get passed over quite a bit is his interaction with Saul just before he went to fight. When David told Saul that he was going to go down to fight against the giant, Saul immediately responded by telling David that he wasn't able to go fight because of his age and lack of experience in comparison to Goliath. Instead of simply accepting the discouragement as truth, David presents his qualifications by reminiscing on when he slayed a lion and a bear while tending to his father's sheep. While this could've been enough to convince some that he was equipped to do what needed to be done, Saul didn't take his word for it and still felt like David needed his input. So, Saul proceeded to place all of his armor on David as his way of further preparing him for battle. The only problem was, the armor was made for Saul, not

David. It didn't fit David and therefore would've been more of a hindrance in the fight than a benefit. Recognizing this, David took the armor off.

In facing whatever giant that stands before you, you can't always listen to what those around you have to say. You will inevitably hear some saying that you can't do what needs to be done or others offering their two cents on how you need to do it. Some may be too afraid to face things themselves, so they transfer their fear and doubt onto you in expectation that you'll cower away as they have. Then of course others feel as if they have what you need in order for you to be victorious and are more than willing to give their advice, most of the time so that they can bring glory to themselves if you come out on top. It's during those times that you may have to pull from your past victories and remind yourself and them of the things God has brought you out of before and this situation will be no different.

The last point that everyone rehearses but doesn't always appreciate is what David used during the battle. After taking off Saul's armor and laying down his sword, David went to a nearby brook and picked up five smooth stones. Armed only with those stones, his sling and the Word of God, he went down to face the giant. While Goliath mocked him and was offended that a kid was sent to fight him, David stood with confidence in what he had to do. He took one of the stones and slung it towards the giant, striking him in the forehead and killing him. After Goliath fell to the ground, David went over and took the giant's own sword out of the holster and cut off his head.

Just like David used what was available to him to kill his giant, the same thing goes for you. You don't need what you think you need, but God will always give you the tools that are necessary. Use what's in your hand and when push comes to shove, you can take the giant's weapons that have formed against you and use them in your favor. It may not be easy but when you understand what lies on the other side of this victory, you won't let anything stand in your way. I didn't and hopefully my journey will inspire you to rise up in the strength that God has given you and slay whatever giant is in your path. If you're like me, your story may be a little different than David's. I didn't have a sling, a stone or a sword... Me? I killed my giant in stilettos.

CHAPTER 1
Fear Had a Grip

"Have I not commanded you? Be strong and courageous. Do not be afraid, do not be discouraged, for the Lord your God will be with you wherever you go." – Joshua 1:9

I remember like it was yesterday. The excitement was in the air. I was a freshman in high school and like all freshmen girls, wanting to be popular and known by the student body. You amped yourself up to participate in whatever club or sport that got the boys' attention, so all the girls who feared tryouts for cheerleading, anxiously gathered and made the decision that we would try out for the flag team.

Every afternoon, we would gather at the football field. Mind you, these were the girls that were not so cute, on the heavy side, nappy hair…just the average chick. Some were outgoing and really had style and rhythm, and there I was, thick glasses, long hair, thunder thighs and a big mouth…oh, and as everybody would say, a pretty face.

So, following the crowd of wild girls, I hung around the gym. I would wait around the locker room to be the last one there, not wanting everyone to notice me. I never wanted the other girls to see me change clothes, fearing they would laugh at me. I would sit in the bathroom stall, on top of the toilet so they couldn't see my feet, and once I heard everyone was gone, I proceeded to dress out. I would begin undressing and pouring sweat at the same time. Rushing to gather with the other girls before I was marked tardy and made to run a lap on the track, I would make my way to the bleachers and the instructor would begin. They started to show us the dance routine and they grouped us by, well…I don't know…"the most likely to make it" squad, to "girl stop, why are you here?" squad. But somewhere between the two, I made the first cut.

As our groups were narrowed down week after week, I still remained, with fear now gripping me every afternoon. I felt like all eyes were on me. Yeah, the chubby one with the pretty face. I was given a flag and ten girls were called to the field. I took my position and with my heart racing, my fingers and hands going numb, my knees feeling like they wouldn't separate, the music started to play. With two voices in my ear, one yelling, "You got this", and the other yelling, "Why are you even up here?" I froze!

Needless to say, tears ran down my face. I couldn't move. My feet felt like two watermelons had been placed on top of them and my sense of movement had been snatched away like a fat kid getting ready to eat a cookie before dinner. I was so embarrassed and knew then that fear had won. Fear had gripped my every thought and caused me to succumb to it. I was stuck. I remembered dropping to my knees and I couldn't stand up. I felt powerless, screaming on the inside but no one was hearing me. As some of my teammates came to help me, others laughed. But being who I was, I cried as if I had just lost someone dear to me. I was escorted off the field and in the background, I could hear the music start up again, not even giving me time to make it back to the locker room. In other words, it felt like I had been played, kicked out, terminated, exposed and just plain humiliated.

About three days later, the team list was posted on the gym door. As I sat and waited for the bell to ring, my mind was flooded with so many emotions but ultimately, I kept telling myself, *"Go ahead and get on the bus…you didn't make it."* When school let out, the crowd rushed to the gym and with knots of nervousness in my stomach, I followed. We all gathered as they were announcing the 1987 Marietta High Flag Team. Again, my heart was racing with a sense of anticipation and hope and as hard as it was to believe, I made the cut. This was my chance to be in the crowd of popular girls, to fit in with the cool kids. It was acceptance on a level I hadn't experienced before. Yes, it was another fearful moment, but a wow moment at the same time.

Sole Nugget:

Even though fear may have a grip on you, don't allow fear to grip you to the point where you say, "The end" before you go through the process. Some of us will already predict an outcome and quit without even trying. Don't quit! Trust God in the process, no matter what's being said or what you may see. Don't allow fear to grip you...grip it!

CHAPTER 2
Fear that Can't Be Ignored

Therefore do not worry about tomorrow, for tomorrow will worry about itself. Each day has enough trouble of its own. – Matthew 6:34

Life is driven by the desire for acceptance and success. We all have said at one time or another that our lives should matter, that we should understand our purpose, that we reach a time where we realize how important we are. Whether we admit it or not, we're all seeking a level of significance that makes our lives more than just mere existence. It's okay to look in the mirror and tell yourself, "You matter".

I had been in this relationship for a short period of time and there was so much that landed me in a fearful, but yet interesting marriage. Not understanding what these emotions on the inside were all about caused me to embrace a strange relationship. Too afraid to talk, to confront, to confess, to communicate, I lived in a situation that caused me to entertain this mental battlefield. So rather than embrace a positive lifestyle that would've forced me to do all the things I feared, I embraced the unknown.

I really thought I could benefit from the choices I had made but those decisions caused a different response. What I thought was love, desire and compassion, ended up being a nightmare on Elm Street. I have to be honest because when you operate in fear, the dead end is closer than you think. I was so ready to invest and commit my whole life to a person that I knew I was very fearful of opening up to. Yes, I went through the whole relationship with tons of unanswered questions, but I couldn't help but think that I was too afraid of the answers to those questions. Meeting family members, expecting him to change, hiding behind allegations, speculations and lots of rumors…ending every conversation with "Che`, you don't see that?". Fearful of what people were saying and because at that time my mother and I weren't on the best of terms, I continued in a toxic, one-sided relationship.

Over 300 invitations were mailed, 16 bridesmaids, wedding reception at the Atlanta Omni, nearly $8,000-$10,000 spent easily, but knowing in my heart that it was not ordained. With the fear of every hand pointing at me, saying "I told you so," I proceeded with the wedding plans even though I knew the relationship was emotionally unhealthy and uncommitted. The big day had arrived and before I knew it, the back doors opened and the pews were filled, the music was playing as the crowd stood up. I began to shake in my satin, ballerina slippers, and the long, vintage gown with lace down my arms and back. A train that looked like it was never-ending followed me as I glided on the rose petal runway. I started crying. Not wanting to look at his handsome face, I kept walking and gazing into the distance. The people on both sides of me began to fade away. Everything became a blur. I closed my eyes as my dad continued to what felt like drag me down the aisle towards the altar, and fear gripped my heart and began squeezing it. I was in a whirlwind of emotions, paralyzed and mad that no one observed my body language but still refusing to interrupt the service. I froze!

So, let's set the record straight. I know I'm not the only one who's been in a relationship and you were fearful of getting out. "Self-revelation does not come easy for some of us"…well let me say ME! Meaning, I'm not the only one who didn't grow up in a house where expression of thoughts was something to embrace or talk about every day. I often, even as a child, overlooked my feelings, denied my feelings and even challenged my own feelings. But this day made me realize that you have to take ownership and speak to the person within. You have to rid your thoughts of other people's opinions, no matter the size of the room. This fear cannot be ignored. So, when the crowd disappeared, and all the decorations were packed away, when there were no more rose petals to walk on and at the end of all the pomp and circumstance, I had a decision to make. Do I continue to ignore all the signs and go on in an unhealthy relationship because I'm too afraid of the alternative, or do I stand up to my fear and do what I know needs to be done? The choice wasn't easy, but it was necessary and after only 8 months of marriage, the gavel in the courtroom sounded and my last name was restored. The fear that I once had was no longer tormenting me. I had been freed.

Sole Nugget:

Many people think that the presence of fear is a negative thing, so they ignore it and refuse to deal with its implications. But experiencing fear is not the problem. It's when we allow that fear to paralyze us, hold us in tumultuous situations and derail us from where we're supposed to be that leaves a lasting scar on our purpose. Never feel guilty for responding to fear, no matter how disappointing it may be. Don't ignore it. Face it and do what needs to be done.

CHAPTER 3
This Fear is No Joke

Even though I walk through the darkest valley,
I will fear no evil, for you are with me, your
rod and your staff, they comfort me. – Psalm
23:4

Born in Marietta at Kennestone Hospital around
3:01am. This 5'6" woman that you see before you
today came into the world a bouncing baby girl with a
head full of hair. When I tell you, I missed being
born on Christmas by 3 days and all my life I hated
my birthday. Everybody was screaming broke from
Christmas or they were getting ready for their big
parties for the new year. So, when I became an adult,
I said that I would make my own celebration. The
norm was to celebrate in church and hang out with
our church family at Shoney's Big Boy, eat the
famous breakfast bar, oh boy, how I loved that bacon,
and end the morning with a hot fudge sundae.

This routine went on for years, until one year I
decided to step out of the box and do something
different. Being new to the club scene, I wanted to
break my tradition. I made up my mind that there
would be no more church for me. So, I started on

Wednesday, laying out what I was going to wear and who I was going to go with. My hairdo was styled by Friday and by 9:00pm, the drinks were flowing. This was my new weekly behavior. My friends and I lived for the weekend and before I knew it, everything I believed in, the appetite I once had for God, was fading away. There were other things, people and places that had gotten my attention. Before I realized it, I had begun to miss a service here and there. At some point, the whole church thing seemed overrated. I still felt at times that I had a close relationship with God, but on Friday nights...babe...the flashing lights, the loud bass from the speakers...this was the life. The rap songs that played in rotation had you moving to the beat as we gathered by the DJ booth...yeah, that was the hotspot. Speaking of DJ booth, when I tell you they knew every weekend that we were coming in, ordering our drinks and hitting the dance floor to the wee hours of the morning. Back then, we could party until the sun came up, you just prayed that the guy you were with had all his teeth and he wasn't your cousin. It was true...one side of Marietta was family with the other side, so you had to be careful or you'd end up being kissing cousins.

So, this one specific encounter, we were walking in ready to have a good time. The music was pumping and we were feeling right, meaning the drinks we had before we entered the club were on point. This little hole in the wall, with one way in and one way out, was jumping. This wasn't my normal, but this particular night we called ourselves club

14

hopping. Sound familiar? Yes, some of y'all are still doing it in the church...church hopping. Anyway! We mingled a little, danced a little and or course, booed up a little. You couldn't help it when the DJ started playing things like "Computer Love" or SWV's "I Get So Weak". And what about "My, My, My" from Johnny Gill or "I'll Make Love to You" by Boyz II Men? Stop the press...Tevin Campbell's "Can We Talk?". Okay, I'm about to stop, but hands down, when I heard "Breaking My Heart" by Mint Condition it was over. And the last one, "Let's Chill" by Guy, if the DJ played this as he announced last call for alcohol, whoever you were with, you knew pretty much he was the one. He had to be the best dude in the house, or at least that's what you were hoping for. If he wasn't, it was truly a Waffle House kind of night.

Okay, back to the story...we were jamming to one of the 90's top hits and there was a loud ruckus around the bar area. I remember people began to scatter. You started hearing the profane words that sounded like they were using a megaphone. People started grabbing bottles and their personal belongings. Girls were screaming and running around trying to find a way out. You had people under the tables, running to the bathroom, it was total chaos. I grabbed about 3 of my girlfriends as we headed for the front door. Can you imagine all of us heading to the door at the same time? The fight didn't stop, it ran into the street. I hid behind a car and started calling on the name of Jesus. I called on Jesus because the fear that came over me at that time was bone-chilling. People were

15

coming out of the club holding their heads, bleeding and crying. As I gathered my thoughts from across the street, I realized then that God had protected me yet again.

Sole Nugget

There are times when the fear that we face is even greater because we know that we're outside of the will of God for our lives. But even when you're in places that you shouldn't be, God has a way of still showing His grace and allowing His protection to overshadow us so that the enemy can't touch us. That's right...CAN'T TOUCH THIS! #hammertime

www.ingramcontent.com/pod-product-compliance
Lightning Source LLC
LaVergne TN
LVHW021615080426
835510LV00019B/2585